50 Decadent Desserts for Chocolate Lovers
Recipes for Home

By: Kelly Johnson

Table of Contents

- Classic Chocolate Lava Cake
- Flourless Chocolate Cake
- Chocolate Mousse
- Triple Chocolate Brownies
- Dark Chocolate Fondue
- Chocolate Chip Cookie Dough Truffles
- Chocolate Tiramisu
- Chocolate Peanut Butter Pie
- Chocolate Silk Pie
- Chocolate Cheesecake
- Chocolate Eclairs
- Black Forest Cake
- Chocolate Pavlova
- Nutella Swirl Brownies
- Chocolate Fudge Cookies
- Chocolate Cupcakes with Ganache
- Salted Caramel Chocolate Tart
- Chocolate Almond Biscotti
- Mocha Chocolate Pudding
- Chocolate-Covered Strawberries
- Chocolate Soufflé
- Rocky Road Fudge
- Chocolate Coconut Macaroons
- S'mores Brownies
- Chocolate Mint Layer Cake
- Chocolate Hazelnut Spread Tart
- Chocolate Banana Bread
- Chocolate-Dipped Pretzels
- White Chocolate Raspberry Cheesecake
- Chocolate Swirl Cheesecake Bars
- Mexican Chocolate Flan
- Chocolate Peanut Butter Cups
- Chocolate Zucchini Bread
- Chocolate Strawberry Shortcake
- Chocolate Chip Pancakes with Syrup

- Espresso Chocolate Cookies
- Chocolate Orange Tart
- Chocolate Cherry Cobbler
- Spicy Hot Chocolate Fudge
- Chocolate Ricotta Cake
- Chocolate Chip Muffins
- Chocolate Scones with Cream
- Chocolate Biscotti with Dipped Ends
- Chocolate Lava Cookies
- Chocolate Mint Brownies
- Chocolate Bourbon Pecan Pie
- Chocolate Pudding Parfaits
- Chocolate Swirled Ice Cream
- Chocolate Almond Torte
- Chocolate Buttercream Frosting

Classic Chocolate Lava Cake

Ingredients

For the cakes:

- 1/2 cup (115g) unsalted butter
- 1 cup (170g) semi-sweet chocolate chips or chopped chocolate
- 2 large eggs
- 2 large egg yolks
- 1/4 cup (50g) granulated sugar
- 2 teaspoons vanilla extract
- 1/4 cup (30g) all-purpose flour
- Pinch of salt

For serving:

- Powdered sugar (for dusting)
- Vanilla ice cream or whipped cream (optional)

Instructions

1. **Preheat the Oven:** Preheat your oven to 425°F (220°C). Grease four ramekins (6 oz size) with butter and dust with cocoa powder to prevent sticking.
2. **Melt Chocolate and Butter:** In a microwave-safe bowl, combine the butter and chocolate. Heat in the microwave in 30-second intervals, stirring after each, until smooth and fully melted.
3. **Mix the Batter:** In a large bowl, whisk together the eggs, egg yolks, and granulated sugar until pale and slightly thickened. Stir in the melted chocolate mixture and vanilla extract until well combined.
4. **Add Dry Ingredients:** Gently fold in the flour and salt until just combined. Be careful not to overmix.
5. **Fill Ramekins:** Divide the batter evenly among the prepared ramekins, filling each about 2/3 full.
6. **Bake:** Place the ramekins on a baking sheet and bake for 12-14 minutes. The edges should be firm, but the center will look soft and slightly jiggly.
7. **Cool and Serve:** Let the cakes cool for 1 minute. Carefully invert each ramekin onto a plate. Gently lift the ramekin off, and the lava cake should come out easily.
8. **Garnish:** Dust with powdered sugar and serve immediately with vanilla ice cream or whipped cream if desired.

Tips

- Serve right away for the best gooey center!
- You can prepare the batter ahead of time and refrigerate it in the ramekins. Just add a couple of extra minutes to the baking time if they're cold.

Enjoy your delicious chocolate lava cakes!

Flourless Chocolate Cake

Ingredients

- 1 cup (170g) semi-sweet or dark chocolate, chopped
- 1/2 cup (115g) unsalted butter
- 3/4 cup (150g) granulated sugar
- 1/4 teaspoon salt
- 1 teaspoon vanilla extract
- 3 large eggs
- 1/2 cup (50g) unsweetened cocoa powder

Instructions

1. Preheat your oven to 375°F (190°C). Grease an 8-inch round cake pan and line the bottom with parchment paper.
2. In a microwave-safe bowl, combine the chocolate and butter. Microwave in 30-second intervals, stirring until melted and smooth.
3. Stir in the sugar, salt, and vanilla. Add the eggs one at a time, mixing well after each addition. Fold in the cocoa powder until just combined.
4. Pour the batter into the prepared pan and bake for 25 minutes. The center should be set but slightly soft.
5. Allow to cool in the pan for 10 minutes, then invert onto a plate. Dust with powdered sugar or cocoa powder before serving.

Chocolate Mousse

Ingredients

- 8 oz (225g) semi-sweet or dark chocolate, chopped
- 3 tablespoons unsalted butter
- 3 large eggs, separated
- 1/4 cup (50g) granulated sugar
- 1 cup (240ml) heavy cream
- 1 teaspoon vanilla extract
- Pinch of salt

Instructions

1. In a heatproof bowl, combine the chocolate and butter. Melt over a pot of simmering water or microwave in 30-second intervals until smooth. Let cool slightly.
2. In a clean bowl, beat the egg whites with a pinch of salt until soft peaks form. Gradually add the sugar and continue to beat until stiff peaks form.
3. In another bowl, whisk the egg yolks into the cooled chocolate mixture until smooth. Gently fold in a third of the whipped egg whites to lighten the mixture, then fold in the remaining egg whites until just combined.
4. In a separate bowl, whip the heavy cream with vanilla until soft peaks form. Gently fold the whipped cream into the chocolate mixture until smooth.
5. Spoon the mousse into individual serving dishes and refrigerate for at least 2 hours before serving.

Triple Chocolate Brownies

Ingredients

- 1/2 cup (115g) unsalted butter
- 1 cup (200g) granulated sugar
- 2 large eggs
- 1 teaspoon vanilla extract
- 1/3 cup (40g) unsweetened cocoa powder
- 1/2 cup (65g) all-purpose flour
- 1/4 teaspoon salt
- 1/4 teaspoon baking powder
- 1/2 cup (90g) semi-sweet chocolate chips
- 1/2 cup (90g) white chocolate chips
- 1/2 cup (90g) milk chocolate chips

Instructions

1. Preheat your oven to 350°F (175°C). Grease an 8x8-inch baking pan.
2. In a medium saucepan, melt the butter over low heat. Remove from heat and stir in the sugar, eggs, and vanilla until smooth.
3. In a separate bowl, whisk together the cocoa powder, flour, salt, and baking powder. Gradually add this mixture to the wet ingredients until just combined.
4. Fold in the semi-sweet, white, and milk chocolate chips until evenly distributed.
5. Pour the batter into the prepared pan and spread evenly. Bake for 20-25 minutes, or until a toothpick inserted in the center comes out with a few moist crumbs.
6. Allow to cool in the pan before cutting into squares. Enjoy!

Enjoy your baking!

Dark Chocolate Fondue

Ingredients

- 8 oz (225g) dark chocolate, chopped
- 1 cup (240ml) heavy cream
- 1 teaspoon vanilla extract
- Dipping items (fresh fruits, marshmallows, pretzels, cookies)

Instructions

1. In a saucepan over medium heat, heat the heavy cream until it just begins to simmer. Remove from heat.
2. Add the chopped dark chocolate and vanilla extract. Let sit for 2-3 minutes, then stir until smooth and fully melted.
3. Transfer to a fondue pot or a serving bowl. Serve with assorted dipping items.

Chocolate Chip Cookie Dough Truffles

Ingredients

- 1/2 cup (115g) unsalted butter, softened
- 1/2 cup (100g) brown sugar
- 1/4 cup (50g) granulated sugar
- 1 teaspoon vanilla extract
- 1 cup (130g) all-purpose flour (heat-treated)
- 1/2 teaspoon salt
- 1/2 cup (90g) mini chocolate chips
- 8 oz (225g) semi-sweet chocolate, for coating

Instructions

1. In a bowl, cream together the butter, brown sugar, granulated sugar, and vanilla until smooth.
2. Gradually mix in the flour and salt, then fold in the mini chocolate chips.
3. Roll the mixture into small balls and place them on a baking sheet. Freeze for about 30 minutes.
4. Melt the semi-sweet chocolate in the microwave. Dip each ball into the chocolate and return to the baking sheet.
5. Refrigerate until the chocolate is set. Enjoy!

Chocolate Tiramisu

Ingredients

- 1 cup (240ml) strong brewed coffee, cooled
- 3 tablespoons coffee liqueur (optional)
- 8 oz (225g) mascarpone cheese
- 1 cup (240ml) heavy cream
- 1/2 cup (60g) powdered sugar
- 1 teaspoon vanilla extract
- 24 ladyfinger cookies
- Unsweetened cocoa powder for dusting

Instructions

1. In a shallow dish, combine the brewed coffee and coffee liqueur.
2. In a bowl, whip the heavy cream with powdered sugar and vanilla until stiff peaks form. Gently fold in the mascarpone until smooth.
3. Quickly dip each ladyfinger into the coffee mixture and layer them in a dish.
4. Spread half of the mascarpone mixture over the ladyfingers. Repeat with another layer of dipped ladyfingers and top with the remaining mascarpone.
5. Refrigerate for at least 4 hours, preferably overnight. Dust with cocoa powder before serving.

Chocolate Peanut Butter Pie

Ingredients

- 1 pre-made graham cracker pie crust
- 1 cup (240ml) heavy cream
- 1 cup (250g) creamy peanut butter
- 1 cup (120g) powdered sugar
- 8 oz (225g) cream cheese, softened
- 1/2 cup (90g) semi-sweet chocolate chips, melted
- Optional: chocolate shavings for garnish

Instructions

1. In a mixing bowl, beat together the peanut butter, cream cheese, and powdered sugar until smooth.
2. In another bowl, whip the heavy cream until soft peaks form. Fold into the peanut butter mixture until well combined.
3. Spread half of the filling into the pie crust. Drizzle melted chocolate on top, then add the remaining filling.
4. Refrigerate for at least 2 hours to set. Garnish with chocolate shavings before serving.

Enjoy your delightful chocolate creations!

Chocolate Silk Pie

Ingredients

- 1 pre-made pie crust (graham cracker or chocolate)
- 6 oz (170g) semi-sweet chocolate, chopped
- 1/4 cup (60ml) heavy cream
- 1 cup (240ml) heavy cream (for whipping)
- 1/2 cup (100g) granulated sugar
- 1 teaspoon vanilla extract
- 3 large eggs
- 1 tablespoon butter

Instructions

1. Preheat your oven to 350°F (175°C). Bake the pie crust according to package instructions if using a raw crust.
2. In a saucepan, melt the chocolate and 1/4 cup of heavy cream over low heat. Stir until smooth, then let cool.
3. In a bowl, beat the eggs and sugar until light and fluffy. Gradually mix in the cooled chocolate and vanilla, followed by the butter.
4. In another bowl, whip the remaining heavy cream until stiff peaks form. Fold it into the chocolate mixture until smooth.
5. Pour into the pie crust and refrigerate for at least 4 hours. Serve chilled.

Chocolate Cheesecake

Ingredients

- 1 1/2 cups (150g) chocolate cookie crumbs
- 1/2 cup (115g) unsalted butter, melted
- 16 oz (450g) cream cheese, softened
- 1 cup (200g) granulated sugar
- 1 teaspoon vanilla extract
- 3 large eggs
- 8 oz (225g) semi-sweet chocolate, melted

Instructions

1. Preheat your oven to 325°F (160°C). Mix the cookie crumbs and melted butter, then press into the bottom of a springform pan.
2. In a bowl, beat the cream cheese, sugar, and vanilla until smooth. Add the eggs one at a time, mixing well after each.
3. Stir in the melted chocolate until fully combined. Pour over the crust.
4. Bake for 50-60 minutes until set. Let cool, then refrigerate for at least 4 hours before serving.

Chocolate Éclairs

Ingredients

- **Choux Pastry:**
    - 1/2 cup (115g) unsalted butter
    - 1 cup (240ml) water
    - 1 cup (125g) all-purpose flour
    - 1/4 teaspoon salt
    - 4 large eggs
- **Chocolate Pastry Cream:**
    - 2 cups (480ml) milk
    - 1/2 cup (100g) granulated sugar
    - 1/4 cup (30g) cornstarch
    - 1/4 teaspoon salt
    - 4 large egg yolks
    - 1 teaspoon vanilla extract
    - 4 oz (115g) semi-sweet chocolate, chopped
- **Chocolate Glaze:**
    - 4 oz (115g) semi-sweet chocolate, chopped
    - 1/4 cup (60ml) heavy cream

Instructions

1. Preheat your oven to 400°F (200°C). In a saucepan, bring butter and water to a boil. Stir in flour and salt, cooking until it forms a ball. Remove from heat and beat in eggs one at a time.
2. Pipe 4-inch lines onto a baking sheet. Bake for 20-25 minutes until golden. Let cool.
3. For the pastry cream, heat milk in a saucepan. In a bowl, whisk sugar, cornstarch, and salt. Gradually add the hot milk. Return to heat and cook until thickened. Stir in egg yolks, then chocolate and vanilla. Cool completely.
4. Fill cooled éclairs with pastry cream. For the glaze, heat cream, pour over chocolate, and stir until smooth. Dip the tops of the éclairs in the glaze.

Black Forest Cake

Ingredients

- **Chocolate Cake:**
    - 1 3/4 cups (220g) all-purpose flour
    - 3/4 cup (65g) unsweetened cocoa powder
    - 2 cups (400g) granulated sugar
    - 1 1/2 teaspoons baking powder
    - 1 1/2 teaspoons baking soda
    - 1 teaspoon salt
    - 2 large eggs
    - 1 cup (240ml) whole milk
    - 1/2 cup (120ml) vegetable oil
    - 2 teaspoons vanilla extract
    - 1 cup (240ml) boiling water
- **Filling:**
    - 2 cups (480ml) heavy cream
    - 1/4 cup (30g) powdered sugar
    - 2 cups (300g) cherry pie filling
- **Garnish:**
    - Chocolate shavings

Instructions

1. Preheat your oven to 350°F (175°C). Grease and flour two 9-inch round cake pans.
2. In a large bowl, mix flour, cocoa powder, sugar, baking powder, baking soda, and salt. Add eggs, milk, oil, and vanilla; mix well. Stir in boiling water.
3. Divide batter between pans and bake for 30-35 minutes. Let cool completely.
4. Whip heavy cream with powdered sugar until stiff peaks form. Place one cake layer on a plate, spread with whipped cream and cherry filling. Top with the second layer and frost the top with remaining whipped cream. Garnish with chocolate shavings.

Chocolate Pavlova

Ingredients

- 4 large egg whites
- 1 cup (200g) granulated sugar
- 1 tablespoon cornstarch
- 1 teaspoon white vinegar
- 2 tablespoons unsweetened cocoa powder
- 1 cup (240ml) heavy cream
- 1 tablespoon powdered sugar
- Fresh berries for topping

Instructions

1. Preheat your oven to 300°F (150°C). Line a baking sheet with parchment paper.
2. In a clean bowl, beat egg whites until soft peaks form. Gradually add sugar, beating until stiff peaks form. Gently fold in cornstarch, vinegar, and cocoa powder.
3. Spoon the mixture onto the parchment, shaping it into a circle with a slight indentation in the center. Bake for 1 hour. Turn off the oven and let it cool completely inside.
4. Whip the cream with powdered sugar until soft peaks form. Top the cooled pavlova with whipped cream and fresh berries.

Nutella Swirl Brownies

Ingredients

- 1/2 cup (115g) unsalted butter
- 1 cup (200g) granulated sugar
- 2 large eggs
- 1 teaspoon vanilla extract
- 1/3 cup (40g) unsweetened cocoa powder
- 1/2 cup (65g) all-purpose flour
- 1/4 teaspoon salt
- 1/4 teaspoon baking powder
- 1/2 cup (150g) Nutella

Instructions

1. Preheat your oven to 350°F (175°C). Grease an 8x8-inch baking pan.
2. Melt the butter in a bowl. Stir in the sugar, then add the eggs and vanilla, mixing well.
3. Add cocoa powder, flour, salt, and baking powder, stirring until just combined.
4. Pour half the batter into the pan, then drop spoonfuls of Nutella on top. Pour the remaining batter and swirl with a knife.
5. Bake for 25-30 minutes. Let cool before cutting into squares.

Chocolate Fudge Cookies

Ingredients

- 1/2 cup (115g) unsalted butter, softened
- 1 cup (200g) brown sugar
- 1/2 cup (100g) granulated sugar
- 2 large eggs
- 1 teaspoon vanilla extract
- 1 cup (130g) all-purpose flour
- 1/2 cup (50g) unsweetened cocoa powder
- 1/2 teaspoon baking soda
- 1/4 teaspoon salt
- 1 cup (180g) semi-sweet chocolate chips

Instructions

1. Preheat your oven to 350°F (175°C). Line a baking sheet with parchment paper.
2. In a bowl, cream together butter, brown sugar, and granulated sugar. Beat in the eggs and vanilla until smooth.
3. In another bowl, whisk together flour, cocoa powder, baking soda, and salt. Gradually add to the wet mixture, then stir in chocolate chips.
4. Drop spoonfuls onto the prepared baking sheet. Bake for 10-12 minutes. Cool on a wire rack.

Chocolate Cupcakes with Ganache

Ingredients

- **Cupcakes:**
    - 1 cup (125g) all-purpose flour
    - 1 cup (200g) granulated sugar
    - 1/3 cup (40g) unsweetened cocoa powder
    - 1 teaspoon baking powder
    - 1/2 teaspoon baking soda
    - 1/4 teaspoon salt
    - 1/2 cup (120ml) whole milk
    - 1/4 cup (60ml) vegetable oil
    - 1 large egg
    - 1 teaspoon vanilla extract
    - 1/2 cup (120ml) boiling water
- **Chocolate Ganache:**
    - 8 oz (225g) semi-sweet chocolate, chopped
    - 1 cup (240ml) heavy cream

Instructions

1. Preheat your oven to 350°F (175°C). Line a cupcake pan with liners.
2. In a bowl, mix flour, sugar, cocoa powder, baking powder, baking soda, and salt. Add milk, oil, egg, and vanilla; mix well. Stir in boiling water.
3. Pour the batter into cupcake liners, filling each about 2/3 full. Bake for 18-20 minutes. Let cool completely.
4. For the ganache, heat the cream until just simmering, then pour over the chopped chocolate. Stir until smooth. Let cool until thickened, then frost the cupcakes.

Enjoy making these delightful chocolate desserts!

Salted Caramel Chocolate Tart

Ingredients

- **Crust:**
    - 1 1/2 cups (150g) chocolate cookie crumbs
    - 1/4 cup (50g) granulated sugar
    - 1/2 cup (115g) unsalted butter, melted
- **Filling:**
    - 1 cup (240ml) heavy cream
    - 8 oz (225g) semi-sweet chocolate, chopped
    - 1/2 cup (120ml) salted caramel sauce
- **Garnish:**
    - Sea salt for sprinkling

Instructions

1. Preheat your oven to 350°F (175°C). Mix cookie crumbs, sugar, and melted butter. Press into a tart pan and bake for 10 minutes. Let cool.
2. In a saucepan, heat the heavy cream until just simmering. Pour over the chopped chocolate, let sit for 2 minutes, then stir until smooth.
3. Stir in the salted caramel sauce. Pour into the cooled crust and refrigerate for at least 2 hours.
4. Before serving, sprinkle with sea salt.

Chocolate Almond Biscotti

Ingredients

- 2 cups (250g) all-purpose flour
- 1 cup (200g) granulated sugar
- 1/3 cup (30g) unsweetened cocoa powder
- 1 teaspoon baking powder
- 1/2 teaspoon salt
- 2 large eggs
- 1 teaspoon vanilla extract
- 1/2 cup (75g) chopped almonds
- 1/2 cup (90g) semi-sweet chocolate chips

Instructions

1. Preheat your oven to 350°F (175°C). Line a baking sheet with parchment paper.
2. In a bowl, whisk together flour, sugar, cocoa powder, baking powder, and salt. In another bowl, whisk eggs and vanilla.
3. Combine wet and dry ingredients, then fold in almonds and chocolate chips. Shape into a log on the baking sheet.
4. Bake for 25 minutes, let cool, then slice into biscotti. Bake slices for an additional 10-12 minutes.

Mocha Chocolate Pudding

Ingredients

- 1/2 cup (100g) granulated sugar
- 1/3 cup (40g) unsweetened cocoa powder
- 1/4 cup (30g) cornstarch
- 1/4 teaspoon salt
- 2 3/4 cups (650ml) milk
- 1 teaspoon vanilla extract
- 1 tablespoon instant coffee granules

Instructions

1. In a saucepan, whisk together sugar, cocoa powder, cornstarch, and salt. Gradually add milk, stirring until smooth.
2. Cook over medium heat, stirring constantly until thickened. Remove from heat and stir in vanilla and coffee.
3. Pour into serving dishes and refrigerate until set, about 2 hours.

Chocolate-Covered Strawberries

Ingredients

- 1 lb (450g) fresh strawberries, washed and dried
- 8 oz (225g) semi-sweet chocolate, chopped
- Optional: white chocolate for drizzling

Instructions

1. Melt the chocolate in a heatproof bowl over simmering water or in the microwave in 30-second intervals.
2. Dip each strawberry into the melted chocolate, allowing excess to drip off. Place on a parchment-lined baking sheet.
3. If desired, melt white chocolate and drizzle over the dipped strawberries. Refrigerate until set.

Chocolate Soufflé

Ingredients

- 2 tablespoons (30g) unsalted butter, for greasing
- 1/3 cup (40g) granulated sugar, plus extra for dusting
- 4 oz (115g) semi-sweet chocolate, chopped
- 2 tablespoons (30ml) milk
- 2 large egg yolks
- 4 large egg whites
- Pinch of salt

Instructions

1. Preheat your oven to 375°F (190°C). Grease ramekins with butter and dust with sugar.
2. Melt chocolate and milk together until smooth. Stir in egg yolks.
3. In another bowl, beat egg whites with salt until stiff peaks form. Gently fold into the chocolate mixture.
4. Divide the mixture among ramekins and bake for 12-15 minutes. Serve immediately.

Rocky Road Fudge

Ingredients

- 2 cups (340g) semi-sweet chocolate chips
- 1 can (14 oz) sweetened condensed milk
- 1 teaspoon vanilla extract
- 1 cup (150g) mini marshmallows
- 1 cup (120g) chopped nuts (walnuts or almonds)

Instructions

1. In a saucepan, melt chocolate chips and sweetened condensed milk over low heat, stirring until smooth. Remove from heat and stir in vanilla.
2. Fold in mini marshmallows and nuts. Pour into a greased 8x8-inch pan and refrigerate until set, about 2 hours. Cut into squares.

Chocolate Coconut Macaroons

Ingredients

- 2 1/2 cups (200g) shredded coconut
- 1/2 cup (100g) granulated sugar
- 1/4 cup (30g) all-purpose flour
- 1/4 teaspoon salt
- 2 large egg whites
- 1 teaspoon vanilla extract
- 4 oz (115g) semi-sweet chocolate, melted (for drizzling)

Instructions

1. Preheat your oven to 325°F (160°C). Line a baking sheet with parchment paper.
2. In a bowl, mix coconut, sugar, flour, and salt. In another bowl, whisk egg whites and vanilla until foamy.
3. Combine the wet and dry ingredients. Drop tablespoon-sized mounds onto the baking sheet.
4. Bake for 20-25 minutes until golden. Drizzle with melted chocolate once cooled.

S'mores Brownies

Ingredients

- **Brownies:**
    - 1/2 cup (115g) unsalted butter
    - 1 cup (200g) granulated sugar
    - 2 large eggs
    - 1 teaspoon vanilla extract
    - 1/3 cup (40g) unsweetened cocoa powder
    - 1/2 cup (65g) all-purpose flour
    - 1/4 teaspoon salt
    - 1/4 teaspoon baking powder
- **Topping:**
    - 1 cup (150g) mini marshmallows
    - 1/2 cup (90g) chocolate chips
    - 1/2 cup (70g) graham cracker crumbs

Instructions

1. Preheat your oven to 350°F (175°C). Grease an 8x8-inch baking pan.
2. Melt butter in a bowl. Stir in sugar, then add eggs and vanilla. Mix in cocoa, flour, salt, and baking powder.
3. Pour the brownie batter into the pan and bake for 20 minutes. Remove from the oven, top with marshmallows, chocolate chips, and graham cracker crumbs.
4. Return to the oven for an additional 5-7 minutes until marshmallows are golden. Let cool before cutting.

Enjoy these delightful chocolate treats!

Chocolate Mint Layer Cake

Ingredients

- **Cake:**
    - 1 3/4 cups (220g) all-purpose flour
    - 3/4 cup (65g) unsweetened cocoa powder
    - 2 cups (400g) granulated sugar
    - 1 1/2 teaspoons baking powder
    - 1 1/2 teaspoons baking soda
    - 1 teaspoon salt
    - 2 large eggs
    - 1 cup (240ml) whole milk
    - 1/2 cup (120ml) vegetable oil
    - 2 teaspoons peppermint extract
    - 1 cup (240ml) boiling water
- **Frosting:**
    - 1 cup (230g) unsalted butter, softened
    - 3 1/2 cups (440g) powdered sugar
    - 1/2 cup (40g) unsweetened cocoa powder
    - 2 tablespoons heavy cream
    - 1 teaspoon peppermint extract
- **Garnish:**
    - Chocolate shavings or mint leaves

Instructions

1. Preheat your oven to 350°F (175°C). Grease and flour two 9-inch round cake pans.
2. In a bowl, mix flour, cocoa powder, sugar, baking powder, baking soda, and salt. Add eggs, milk, oil, and peppermint extract; mix well. Stir in boiling water.
3. Divide batter between pans and bake for 30-35 minutes. Let cool completely.
4. For the frosting, beat butter until creamy. Gradually add powdered sugar and cocoa, then mix in cream and peppermint extract until fluffy.
5. Frost the cooled cake and garnish with chocolate shavings or mint leaves.

Chocolate Hazelnut Spread Tart

Ingredients

- **Crust:**
    - 1 1/2 cups (150g) chocolate cookie crumbs
    - 1/4 cup (50g) granulated sugar
    - 1/2 cup (115g) unsalted butter, melted
- **Filling:**
    - 1 cup (240ml) heavy cream
    - 1 cup (280g) chocolate hazelnut spread
    - 4 oz (115g) cream cheese, softened
- **Topping:**
    - Chopped hazelnuts
    - Chocolate shavings

Instructions

1. Preheat your oven to 350°F (175°C). Mix cookie crumbs, sugar, and melted butter. Press into a tart pan and bake for 10 minutes. Let cool.
2. In a bowl, whip the heavy cream until soft peaks form. In another bowl, beat the cream cheese until smooth, then mix in the chocolate hazelnut spread.
3. Gently fold in the whipped cream until combined. Pour into the cooled crust and refrigerate for at least 2 hours.
4. Top with chopped hazelnuts and chocolate shavings before serving.

Chocolate Banana Bread

Ingredients

- 1 1/2 cups (190g) all-purpose flour
- 1/2 cup (40g) unsweetened cocoa powder
- 1 teaspoon baking soda
- 1/2 teaspoon salt
- 1/2 cup (115g) unsalted butter, softened
- 1 cup (200g) granulated sugar
- 2 large eggs
- 3 ripe bananas, mashed
- 1 teaspoon vanilla extract
- 1/2 cup (90g) chocolate chips

Instructions

1. Preheat your oven to 350°F (175°C). Grease a 9x5-inch loaf pan.
2. In a bowl, whisk together flour, cocoa powder, baking soda, and salt. In another bowl, cream butter and sugar until light and fluffy.
3. Beat in eggs, then add mashed bananas and vanilla. Gradually mix in dry ingredients until just combined. Fold in chocolate chips.
4. Pour batter into the prepared pan and bake for 60-70 minutes. Let cool before slicing.

Chocolate-Dipped Pretzels

Ingredients

- 1 bag (10 oz) pretzel rods or twists
- 8 oz (225g) semi-sweet chocolate, chopped
- Optional toppings: sprinkles, crushed nuts, sea salt

Instructions

1. Melt the chocolate in a heatproof bowl over simmering water or in the microwave in 30-second intervals until smooth.
2. Dip each pretzel into the chocolate, letting excess drip off. Place on a parchment-lined baking sheet.
3. While still wet, sprinkle with desired toppings. Refrigerate until chocolate is set.

White Chocolate Raspberry Cheesecake

Ingredients

- **Crust:**
    - 1 1/2 cups (150g) graham cracker crumbs
    - 1/2 cup (115g) unsalted butter, melted
    - 1/4 cup (50g) granulated sugar
- **Filling:**
    - 16 oz (450g) cream cheese, softened
    - 1 cup (200g) granulated sugar
    - 3 large eggs
    - 1 teaspoon vanilla extract
    - 8 oz (225g) white chocolate, melted
    - 1 cup (240ml) raspberry puree (fresh or frozen)

Instructions

1. Preheat your oven to 325°F (160°C). Mix crust ingredients and press into the bottom of a 9-inch springform pan. Bake for 10 minutes.
2. In a bowl, beat cream cheese and sugar until smooth. Add eggs one at a time, then vanilla and melted white chocolate.
3. Pour half the filling into the crust, then drizzle raspberry puree. Pour remaining filling on top and swirl with a knife.
4. Bake for 55-60 minutes. Let cool, then refrigerate for at least 4 hours before serving.

Chocolate Swirl Cheesecake Bars

Ingredients

- **Crust:**
    - 1 1/2 cups (150g) chocolate cookie crumbs
    - 1/4 cup (50g) granulated sugar
    - 1/2 cup (115g) unsalted butter, melted
- **Filling:**
    - 16 oz (450g) cream cheese, softened
    - 3/4 cup (150g) granulated sugar
    - 3 large eggs
    - 1 teaspoon vanilla extract
    - 1/2 cup (90g) semi-sweet chocolate, melted

Instructions

1. Preheat your oven to 325°F (160°C). Line an 8x8-inch baking pan with parchment paper.
2. Mix crust ingredients and press into the bottom of the pan. Bake for 10 minutes.
3. In a bowl, beat cream cheese and sugar until smooth. Add eggs one at a time, then vanilla.
4. Pour half the filling over the crust, then swirl in melted chocolate. Pour remaining filling and swirl again.
5. Bake for 30-35 minutes. Let cool, then refrigerate for at least 2 hours before cutting into bars.

Mexican Chocolate Flan

Ingredients

- **Flan:**
    - 1 cup (200g) granulated sugar (for caramel)
    - 1 can (14 oz) sweetened condensed milk
    - 1 can (12 oz) evaporated milk
    - 3 large eggs
    - 1 teaspoon vanilla extract
    - 2 tablespoons unsweetened cocoa powder
    - 1 teaspoon ground cinnamon
- **Garnish:**
    - Whipped cream and chocolate shavings (optional)

Instructions

1. Preheat your oven to 350°F (175°C). In a saucepan, melt sugar over medium heat until golden. Quickly pour into a round flan mold.
2. In a blender, combine condensed milk, evaporated milk, eggs, vanilla, cocoa powder, and cinnamon. Blend until smooth.
3. Pour the mixture over the caramelized sugar. Place the mold in a baking dish and fill the dish with hot water halfway up the sides of the mold.
4. Bake for 50-60 minutes. Let cool, then refrigerate for at least 4 hours. Invert onto a plate before serving.

Chocolate Peanut Butter Cups

Ingredients

- 1 cup (175g) semi-sweet chocolate chips
- 1/2 cup (125g) creamy peanut butter
- 1/4 cup (30g) powdered sugar
- Mini cupcake liners

Instructions

1. Melt half the chocolate chips in a microwave or double boiler. Spoon a small amount into each cupcake liner and spread to coat the bottom.
2. In a bowl, mix peanut butter and powdered sugar until smooth. Spoon a small dollop onto the chocolate in each liner.
3. Melt the remaining chocolate chips and pour over the peanut butter, sealing the cups. Refrigerate until set.

Enjoy these delicious chocolate creations!

Chocolate Zucchini Bread

Ingredients

- 1 1/2 cups (190g) all-purpose flour
- 1/2 cup (50g) unsweetened cocoa powder
- 1 teaspoon baking soda
- 1/2 teaspoon salt
- 1 teaspoon cinnamon
- 1/2 cup (115g) unsalted butter, melted
- 1 cup (200g) granulated sugar
- 2 large eggs
- 1 teaspoon vanilla extract
- 1 1/2 cups (150g) grated zucchini
- 1/2 cup (90g) chocolate chips

Instructions

1. Preheat your oven to 350°F (175°C). Grease a 9x5-inch loaf pan.
2. In a bowl, whisk together flour, cocoa powder, baking soda, salt, and cinnamon.
3. In another bowl, mix melted butter and sugar. Add eggs and vanilla, then stir in zucchini.
4. Gradually add dry ingredients, folding in chocolate chips. Pour batter into the prepared pan.
5. Bake for 50-60 minutes. Let cool before slicing.

Chocolate Strawberry Shortcake

Ingredients

- **Cake:**
    - 1 1/2 cups (190g) all-purpose flour
    - 1/2 cup (100g) granulated sugar
    - 1/4 cup (25g) unsweetened cocoa powder
    - 1 1/2 teaspoons baking powder
    - 1/2 teaspoon baking soda
    - 1/4 teaspoon salt
    - 1/2 cup (115g) unsalted butter, softened
    - 2 large eggs
    - 1 teaspoon vanilla extract
    - 1/2 cup (120ml) buttermilk
- **Toppings:**
    - 2 cups (300g) sliced strawberries
    - 1 cup (240ml) heavy cream
    - 2 tablespoons powdered sugar

Instructions

1. Preheat your oven to 350°F (175°C). Grease and flour two 9-inch round cake pans.
2. In a bowl, mix flour, sugar, cocoa, baking powder, baking soda, and salt. Add butter, eggs, vanilla, and buttermilk; mix until smooth.
3. Divide batter between pans and bake for 25-30 minutes. Let cool completely.
4. Whip cream with powdered sugar until soft peaks form. Place one cake layer on a plate, top with strawberries and whipped cream, then add the second layer and repeat.

Chocolate Chip Pancakes with Syrup

Ingredients

- 1 cup (125g) all-purpose flour
- 2 tablespoons (25g) granulated sugar
- 2 teaspoons baking powder
- 1/2 teaspoon salt
- 1 cup (240ml) milk
- 1 large egg
- 2 tablespoons (30g) unsalted butter, melted
- 1/2 cup (90g) chocolate chips
- Maple syrup for serving

Instructions

1. In a bowl, whisk together flour, sugar, baking powder, and salt. In another bowl, mix milk, egg, and melted butter.
2. Combine wet and dry ingredients, then fold in chocolate chips.
3. Heat a skillet over medium heat. Pour 1/4 cup of batter for each pancake. Cook until bubbles form, then flip and cook until golden.
4. Serve with maple syrup.

Espresso Chocolate Cookies

Ingredients

- 1 cup (115g) all-purpose flour
- 1/2 cup (50g) unsweetened cocoa powder
- 1 teaspoon baking powder
- 1/4 teaspoon salt
- 1/2 cup (115g) unsalted butter, softened
- 1 cup (200g) granulated sugar
- 1 large egg
- 1 teaspoon vanilla extract
- 1 tablespoon instant espresso powder
- 1/2 cup (90g) chocolate chips

Instructions

1. Preheat your oven to 350°F (175°C). Line a baking sheet with parchment paper.
2. In a bowl, whisk together flour, cocoa powder, baking powder, and salt.
3. In another bowl, beat butter and sugar until creamy. Add egg, vanilla, and espresso powder; mix well.
4. Gradually add dry ingredients, then fold in chocolate chips. Drop spoonfuls onto the baking sheet.
5. Bake for 10-12 minutes. Let cool before enjoying.

Chocolate Orange Tart

Ingredients

- **Crust:**
    - 1 1/2 cups (150g) chocolate cookie crumbs
    - 1/4 cup (50g) granulated sugar
    - 1/2 cup (115g) unsalted butter, melted
- **Filling:**
    - 8 oz (225g) semi-sweet chocolate, chopped
    - 1/2 cup (120ml) heavy cream
    - 1/4 cup (60ml) orange juice
    - 1 teaspoon orange zest
    - 2 large eggs

Instructions

1. Preheat your oven to 350°F (175°C). Mix cookie crumbs, sugar, and melted butter. Press into a tart pan and bake for 10 minutes. Let cool.
2. In a saucepan, heat heavy cream until simmering. Pour over chopped chocolate; let sit for 2 minutes, then stir until smooth.
3. Stir in orange juice, zest, and eggs until combined. Pour into the crust and bake for 20-25 minutes. Let cool before serving.

Chocolate Cherry Cobbler

Ingredients

- **Filling:**
    - 2 cups (300g) fresh or frozen cherries, pitted
    - 1/4 cup (50g) granulated sugar
    - 1 tablespoon cornstarch
    - 1 tablespoon lemon juice
- **Topping:**
    - 1 cup (125g) all-purpose flour
    - 1/2 cup (100g) granulated sugar
    - 1/4 cup (25g) unsweetened cocoa powder
    - 1 teaspoon baking powder
    - 1/4 teaspoon salt
    - 1/2 cup (120ml) milk
    - 1/4 cup (60g) unsalted butter, melted

Instructions

1. Preheat your oven to 350°F (175°C). In a bowl, combine cherries, sugar, cornstarch, and lemon juice. Pour into a baking dish.
2. In another bowl, whisk together flour, sugar, cocoa powder, baking powder, and salt. Stir in milk and melted butter until combined.
3. Pour batter over the cherry filling. Bake for 30-35 minutes until the top is set. Serve warm.

Spicy Hot Chocolate Fudge

Ingredients

- 2 cups (340g) semi-sweet chocolate chips
- 1 can (14 oz) sweetened condensed milk
- 1 teaspoon vanilla extract
- 1/2 teaspoon ground cinnamon
- 1/4 teaspoon cayenne pepper (adjust to taste)
- Pinch of salt

Instructions

1. In a saucepan, melt chocolate chips and sweetened condensed milk over low heat, stirring until smooth.
2. Remove from heat and stir in vanilla, cinnamon, cayenne pepper, and salt.
3. Pour into a greased 8x8-inch pan and refrigerate until set, about 2 hours. Cut into squares.

Chocolate Ricotta Cake

Ingredients

- 1 1/2 cups (190g) all-purpose flour
- 1/2 cup (50g) unsweetened cocoa powder
- 1 teaspoon baking powder
- 1/2 teaspoon baking soda
- 1/4 teaspoon salt
- 1 cup (240ml) ricotta cheese
- 1 cup (200g) granulated sugar
- 1/2 cup (120ml) vegetable oil
- 2 large eggs
- 1 teaspoon vanilla extract
- 1/2 cup (90g) chocolate chips

Instructions

1. Preheat your oven to 350°F (175°C). Grease a 9-inch round cake pan.
2. In a bowl, whisk together flour, cocoa powder, baking powder, baking soda, and salt.
3. In another bowl, mix ricotta, sugar, oil, eggs, and vanilla until smooth. Gradually add dry ingredients, then fold in chocolate chips.
4. Pour batter into the prepared pan and bake for 30-35 minutes. Let cool before slicing.

Enjoy these delightful chocolate recipes!

Chocolate Chip Muffins

Ingredients

- 2 cups (250g) all-purpose flour
- 1 cup (200g) granulated sugar
- 1 tablespoon baking powder
- 1/2 teaspoon salt
- 1/2 cup (120ml) vegetable oil
- 1 cup (240ml) milk
- 2 large eggs
- 1 teaspoon vanilla extract
- 1 cup (175g) chocolate chips

Instructions

1. Preheat your oven to 375°F (190°C). Line a muffin tin with paper liners.
2. In a bowl, mix flour, sugar, baking powder, and salt. In another bowl, whisk together oil, milk, eggs, and vanilla.
3. Combine wet and dry ingredients until just mixed. Fold in chocolate chips.
4. Fill muffin liners about 2/3 full and bake for 18-20 minutes. Let cool before serving.

Chocolate Scones with Cream

Ingredients

- 2 cups (250g) all-purpose flour
- 1/2 cup (50g) unsweetened cocoa powder
- 1/4 cup (50g) granulated sugar
- 1 tablespoon baking powder
- 1/2 teaspoon salt
- 1/2 cup (115g) cold unsalted butter, cubed
- 1/2 cup (120ml) heavy cream
- 1 teaspoon vanilla extract
- 1/2 cup (90g) chocolate chips

Instructions

1. Preheat your oven to 400°F (200°C). Line a baking sheet with parchment paper.
2. In a bowl, mix flour, cocoa powder, sugar, baking powder, and salt. Cut in butter until crumbly.
3. Stir in cream, vanilla, and chocolate chips until a dough forms. Turn onto a floured surface, shape into a circle, and cut into wedges.
4. Bake for 15-20 minutes. Serve warm with whipped cream.

Chocolate Biscotti with Dipped Ends

Ingredients

- 2 cups (250g) all-purpose flour
- 1/2 cup (50g) unsweetened cocoa powder
- 1 cup (200g) granulated sugar
- 1 teaspoon baking powder
- 1/2 teaspoon salt
- 3 large eggs
- 1 teaspoon vanilla extract
- 1 cup (150g) chocolate chips (for dipping)

Instructions

1. Preheat your oven to 350°F (175°C). Line a baking sheet with parchment paper.
2. In a bowl, mix flour, cocoa powder, sugar, baking powder, and salt. In another bowl, whisk eggs and vanilla.
3. Combine wet and dry ingredients to form a dough. Shape into a log on the baking sheet and bake for 25 minutes.
4. Let cool, then slice into biscotti and bake again for 10-15 minutes. Dip ends in melted chocolate and let set.

Chocolate Lava Cookies

Ingredients

- 1 cup (175g) semi-sweet chocolate chips
- 1/2 cup (115g) unsalted butter
- 1 cup (200g) granulated sugar
- 2 large eggs
- 1 teaspoon vanilla extract
- 1/2 cup (65g) all-purpose flour
- 1/4 teaspoon salt

Instructions

1. Preheat your oven to 350°F (175°C). Grease a baking sheet.
2. Melt chocolate and butter together in a bowl. Stir in sugar, then add eggs and vanilla. Mix in flour and salt until just combined
3. Drop spoonfuls onto the baking sheet and bake for 10-12 minutes. The centers should be soft. Let cool slightly before serving.

Chocolate Mint Brownies

Ingredients

- **Brownie Base:**
    - 1 cup (225g) unsalted butter
    - 2 cups (400g) granulated sugar
    - 4 large eggs
    - 1 teaspoon vanilla extract
    - 1 cup (130g) all-purpose flour
    - 1 cup (90g) unsweetened cocoa powder
    - 1/2 teaspoon salt
- **Mint Frosting:**
    - 1/2 cup (115g) unsalted butter, softened
    - 2 cups (240g) powdered sugar
    - 2 tablespoons milk
    - 1 teaspoon peppermint extract
- **Chocolate Ganache:**
    - 1 cup (175g) semi-sweet chocolate chips
    - 1/2 cup (120ml) heavy cream

Instructions

1. Preheat your oven to 350°F (175°C). Grease a 9x13-inch baking pan.
2. Melt butter and mix with sugar. Add eggs and vanilla, then stir in flour, cocoa, and salt.
3. Pour into the pan and bake for 25-30 minutes. Let cool.
4. For the frosting, beat butter, powdered sugar, milk, and peppermint extract until smooth. Spread over cooled brownies.
5. For ganache, heat cream and pour over chocolate chips. Stir until smooth, then pour over frosting. Let set before cutting.

Chocolate Pudding Parfaits

Ingredients

- **Chocolate Pudding:**
    - 1/2 cup (100g) granulated sugar
    - 1/3 cup (40g) unsweetened cocoa powder
    - 1/4 cup (30g) cornstarch
    - 1/4 teaspoon salt
    - 2 3/4 cups (650ml) milk
    - 1 teaspoon vanilla extract
- **For Assembly:**
    - Whipped cream
    - Chocolate shavings or crushed cookies

Instructions

1. In a saucepan, whisk together sugar, cocoa, cornstarch, and salt. Gradually add milk, stirring until smooth.
2. Cook over medium heat, stirring constantly until thickened. Remove from heat and stir in vanilla.
3. Pour pudding into cups and chill for at least 2 hours. Layer with whipped cream and top with chocolate shavings before serving.

Chocolate Swirled Ice Cream

Ingredients

- 2 cups (480ml) heavy cream
- 1 cup (240ml) whole milk
- 3/4 cup (150g) granulated sugar
- 1 teaspoon vanilla extract
- 1 cup (175g) semi-sweet chocolate, melted

Instructions

1. In a bowl, whisk together cream, milk, sugar, and vanilla until sugar is dissolved.
2. Pour mixture into an ice cream maker and churn according to manufacturer's instructions.
3. When ice cream is almost ready, slowly drizzle in melted chocolate and swirl with a spoon.
4. Transfer to a container and freeze for at least 4 hours before serving.

Enjoy these delicious chocolate treats!

Chocolate Almond Torte

Ingredients

- 1 cup (100g) almond flour
- 1/2 cup (50g) unsweetened cocoa powder
- 1 teaspoon baking powder
- 1/4 teaspoon salt
- 1/2 cup (115g) unsalted butter, softened
- 3/4 cup (150g) granulated sugar
- 3 large eggs
- 1 teaspoon vanilla extract
- 1/4 cup (60ml) brewed coffee (optional)

Instructions

1. Preheat your oven to 350°F (175°C). Grease an 8-inch round cake pan and line the bottom with parchment paper.
2. In a bowl, whisk together almond flour, cocoa powder, baking powder, and salt.
3. In a separate bowl, cream together butter and sugar until light and fluffy. Add eggs one at a time, mixing well after each addition. Stir in vanilla and coffee.
4. Gradually add the dry ingredients to the wet mixture, mixing until just combined.
5. Pour the batter into the prepared pan and smooth the top. Bake for 25-30 minutes, or until a toothpick inserted in the center comes out clean.
6. Let the torte cool in the pan for 10 minutes, then transfer to a wire rack to cool completely.

Chocolate Buttercream Frosting

Ingredients

- 1 cup (230g) unsalted butter, softened
- 3 1/2 cups (440g) powdered sugar
- 1/2 cup (50g) unsweetened cocoa powder
- 1/4 cup (60ml) heavy cream
- 1 teaspoon vanilla extract
- Pinch of salt

Instructions

1. In a large bowl, beat the softened butter until creamy and smooth.
2. Gradually add powdered sugar and cocoa powder, mixing on low speed until combined.
3. Pour in heavy cream, vanilla extract, and salt. Beat on medium speed for 2-3 minutes, until the frosting is light and fluffy.
4. Adjust consistency by adding more cream or powdered sugar if needed.
5. Frost the cooled chocolate almond torte as desired.

Enjoy your delicious chocolate almond torte topped with creamy chocolate buttercream!

www.ingramcontent.com/pod-product-compliance
Lightning Source LLC
LaVergne TN
LVHW081335060526
838201LV00055B/2659